# Armies of the Heavens: Divine Help in Wars

**End Times, Rise of Antichrist (Dajjal), and Golden Age**

ahmet yazici

Published by ahmet yazici, 2022.

While every precaution has been taken in the preparation of this book, the publisher assumes no responsibility for errors or omissions, or for damages resulting from the use of the information contained herein.

ARMIES OF THE HEAVENS: DIVINE HELP IN WARS

**First edition. October 19, 2022.**



ISBN: 979-8215672099

Written by ahmet yazici.

# Also by ahmet yazici

**A Glimpse into How the Universe Works**
Big Crunch: Invisible Apocalyptic Machines
An Islamic Approach to Time Travel


**A Glimpse into the Unseen Realms**
Unmaterial Molds
How to Understand the Soul: Spirit or Brain?
How Can Soothsayers Predict the Future?


**End Times, Rise of Antichrist (Dajjal), and Golden Age**
The Return of Jesus: Conquest of Rome
Armies of the Heavens: Divine Help in Wars


**Standalone**
Can God Create a Rock He Cannot Lift?: Omnipotence
Paradox

Wouldn't Eternal Life in Paradise Be Boring?: Life in Heaven
Do Humans and Apes Have the Same Ancestors?: Evolution
and Creation in Light of Striking Similarities
Do All Uncovered Women Go to Hell?
Is Coronavirus a Divine Warning?
Is the Quran the Word of God?
Who Created the Mobile Phone?
Why Did Islamic Countries Lag Behind?: Is Islam Not the
Right Religion?

# Table of Contents

To Muhammad Samir and Ahmad Shakir, Engin
Demir, Bedirhan Kaldirim, Adem Kandemir...

# Prologue

This book should not be viewed as a political work. Some issues could not be explained without touching (a little) politics. The brothers/sisters, who are distant from politics, will agree with me when they read the book. I wish I didn't get into the political issues at all. However, in this case, our issue would not be fully understood.

It is impossible not to mention the names of the states when referring to politics. I've not mentioned these countries with any hostile or grudge-bearing sentiment. I am not the enemy of any country or nation. Also, the mistakes of one person cannot be attributed to the whole nation... Churchill's sins cannot be attributed to the entire English nation.

In this work, I gave examples from the Ottoman Empire and Turkey. My aim is not to be nationalistic. Racism is when a nation sees its own race as superior because of its blood. Nation, race is a fact. That's why every nation can love them by talking about the virtues of their own nation. I am proud of the Turkish nation for its service to Islam. This pride and love come from faith. But if I separate Islam and the Turkish nation and see the Turkish nation as superior only because of its blood, this is negative nationalism and there is no place for negative nationalism in Islam. No nation has any superiority over another nation. Superiority is based on piety. In this respect, a pious Muslim of French origin is superior to a sinful Turk. Let me add that if I were not Turkish, I would still be proud of whichever nation served Islam. If I were a French Muslim, I would still be proud of the Turkish nation on behalf of Islam... Genghis Khan is Turkish. But I hate him. Because he has done great harm to Islam...

Ottoman can be criticized. However, a Muslim cannot be an enemy of the Ottoman Empire. If a person is not an enemy of the Ottomans because of his ignorance, he is an enemy of the Ottomans because there is a mistake in his creed. Because Ottoman is the castle of ahlus sunnah. I especially warn my brothers/sisters who chose Islam later on this issue.

The Ottoman Empire has many aspects to criticize. One of them was that the Ottomans prevented some scientific studies. For example, the destruction of the Takiyuddin Observatory. Takiyyuddin Mehmed bin Maruf wanted to open an Observatory in Istanbul and faced many obstacles. In the end, the opposition won and this Observatory was destroyed. The reason was the thought that acquiring information about the future would bring bad luck to the state. Chief Astrologer Takiyyuddin was a first in this regard. His observatory was 10 years ahead of the observatory established by Tycho-Brahe in Europe with the encouragement of King Frederick II of Denmark...

The persons or communities in question are those who are hostile to the Ottoman Empire. An imam or community in Germany or Australia has the right not to be interested in the Ottoman Empire. Or he may have never heard of the Ottomans because knowing the Ottomans is not one of the commandments of Islam. Or, there is no need for a religious scholar or sheikh of any country to talk about the Ottoman Empire. Or they have the right to criticize the mistakes of the Ottomans. I'm not making any claims that these are outside the ahlus sunnah wal jamaah circle. However, people who denigrate the Ottoman and/or other Muslim Turkish states in their conversations, accuse them of infidelity and always talk about their bad sides should be avoided. Again, I warn my brothers or sisters, who have just met Islam, about these people or communities.

I will give some information about Turkey and the Turkish people. I share this information, which even most Turkish people do not care about, so you can better understand the subject. After reading this work patiently, you will realize the manifestations of divine will.

I had two main purposes in this work. One is wisdom, the other is faith. I've tried to evaluate the events from the point of view of wisdom. I've also discussed the aspects of the events related to faith.

For example, according to Islamic creed, angels are not daughters of Allah. Everybody knows this. However, some do not know the fact that angels are not helpers of Allah.

In this work, I will not give specific information that does not cause doubts and delusions and is easily confirmed. For example, I will not talk about the archangels.

# Nations

There are different ways of looking at things. One is the apparent look. The common people look at the apparent. They make an evaluation and a statement of opinion, according to their view, ingenuity, and knowledge. The rate of hitting in this may be at utmost forty percent. Because appearances deceive. Trying to explain things by looking at the reasons deceives people.

The second group includes the following: Those who initiate the causes, are the source of the causes, direct the perception operations, make plans and programs, want to get results with the project they put forward, and want to direct humanity, nations, and politics. These are the great states, the wealthy, and especially the Jews. Their right to hit in an issue goes up to 60-70%. Because they move the causes, work, plan, and schedule, so Allah helps them. God helps those who work and fulfill the causes.

They use their right to oppression. They use it to oppress the oppressed and for their own benefit. But God gives them respite. He does not determine the outcome as they wish. Giving respite doesn't mean leaving the world to them completely. That respite means giving time for the believers to wake up, for the right power to be vigilant and strengthened, and to make an adjustment... Their right to make the right decision and to know the result correctly is 60-70 percent. They are in charge and they do the planning. By looking at these, those who comment on the events knowing their plans can get as accurate results as they do.

There is also a deep plan. We call it destiny's plan. We call it God's will. Those who put forth the reasons are not strong enough against this plan. The common people also do not have the right to pass to that area. This is the plan of destiny determined by Allah. Only close servants in the sight of Allah can know this. They explain the issue to some interlocutors and pass it on as much as they deem necessary. Not everyone may be aware of this, but if competent people and those who know these individuals realize this secret plan of destiny and interpret them accordingly, time does not disprove them, but confirms them. Even if the plan of the People of Aberration and the projects they put forward are outwardly realized, it gives strength and power to the plan that Allah has worked on secretly and deeply and cannot stop it.

We call it Jalali and Jamali manifestation. The day is Jamali, the night is Jalali. Summer is jamali, winter is jalali. Peace is jamali, war is jalali. If it is always day and summer, the balance is disturbed. This also applies to believers and disbelievers. Believers don't always win. Otherwise, the balance and order will be disturbed.

*Reasons for the Rise of the Jews*

Jews were expelled from Palestine by the Romans towards the middle of the 5th century AD. After the Roman Empire accepted Christianity, he expelled the Jews by saying, "You crucified our prophet." (Actually, Jesus (PBUH) was not crucified and was not killed. He ascended to heaven. He will descend to earth again.) The Jews were expelled on the condition that they go out of the Roman territory. For this reason, the Jews go to Russia, Spain, Germany, and England, which were not in Roman hands at that time. But the lands they went to also became Christians. For this reason, the Jews could not live in small settlements. Undesirable people cannot live in small settlements where everyone knows each other. However, they can live in large and crowded cities that are suitable for cosmopolitanism. They lived in big and crowded cities. In big cities, military service and civil service were forbidden for them. This role that their enemies have assigned to them has enabled them to rise by chance. Not because of the intelligence of the Jew. They have two jobs left. Science and commerce. Large cities are the most suitable places for great trade and education. In addition, the Jews took the privilege of being divided families. If a Jew settled in Berlin, one of his relatives settled in Paris and another in London. These families had the opportunity to exploit the nations in a very short time with the efficiency of international cooperation by entering into an international relationship. They also benefited from being divided families. However, this is not something they think about.

Those who see the distance they have covered and the result they have reached, believe in an extraordinariness in the Jews. This is wrong. The factors that rose them arose out of the role their enemies assigned them. If they lived in villages and occupied the land, at least half of their population would remain peasants. Big cities gave them the opportunity to study and trade. However, the Europeans put some obstacles in front of them to prevent them from getting a full result from this education and trade.

Jews could only live in the suburbs of metropolitan cities. They could do things like rag collection. They switched from rag shops to antiques. They moved from antiques to money changers and bankers. And the conditions in Europe enabled the Jews to add wealth to their wealth.

Let me say this much about the education of the Jews. Those who were educated mostly dealt with social sciences. Behind all the philosophical currents that corrupt humanity are Jewish philosophers. But there are no Jews in technical discoveries. The Jews have acquired the sciences that affect the course of social events that affect people's brains and direction. They dealt with the fields of history and sociology, especially philosophy.

No Jew follows these Jewish philosophers. The Jews propound these philosophical ideas for others. The Jews become the head, the brain, and corrupt other people. Because they want all humanity to serve the Jews.

Destiny's plan intended the rise of the Jewish nation. Thus, the state of Israel was established. Allah had declared in the Qur'an that He would raise the Jews. Here is the relevant quote from my book "The Return of Jesus":

*Since the second corruption and rise of Jews manifest itself as the state of Israel, the end of Israel will be as stated in the Quran:*

*And We conveyed to the Children of Israel in the Scripture that, "You will surely cause corruption on the earth twice, and you will surely reach [a degree of] great haughtiness. So when the [time of] promise came for the first of them, We sent against you servants of Ours - those of great military might, and they probed [even] into the homes, and it was a promise fulfilled. Then We gave back to you a return victory over them. And We reinforced you with wealth and sons and made you more numerous in manpower. [And said], "If you do good, you do good for yourselves; and if you do evil, [you do it] to yourselves." Then when the final promise came, [We sent your enemies] to sadden your faces and to enter the temple in Jerusalem, as they entered it the first time, and to destroy what they had taken over with [total] destruction. (Al-Isra 17:4-7)*

*So then why do Jews not take a blow in Palestine? As Badiuzzaman says, they will take a blow; however, it is being postponed because of their respect for the Prophets. They value the Prophets of the children of Israel, and they want to stay on that land by carrying their religious, divine, and national feelings. They say: "Our Prophets lived on these lands and are buried here." In addition, since the Jews regret and repent, Allah may have given them strength and state.*

When Turkey takes over the leadership of the Islamic world and the task of jihad, if the state of Israel continues its corruption, it will certainly receive the punishment it deserves by the Turkish army, which is described as the sharp sword of Islam.

The Jewish nation has an essential place in the strife of the End Times. The Qur'an addresses to all times. Today, there are people who represent the Pharaoh and try to keep his life view and ideas alive. Likewise, Moses (PBUH) is not on earth today, but there is someone who represents that blessed person. In other words, there are people who imitate the methods of Moses (PBUH) in the war against the Pharaohs of this time and are armed with the weapon of that blessed person. For example, Today's Pharaohs also use magic as a weapon. Of course, the Qur'an's address to all times is not limited to Pharaoh and Moses (PBUH).

The Qur'an frequently mentions the sons of Israel. The Qur'an has included the historical events because it will always repeat itself. One of the most important pieces of wisdom in giving a lot of space to the sons of Israel is the negative roles they will assume throughout history. Systems such as interest, capitalism, and materialism are the products of Jewish mind. Wherever they are, they set up secret committees and start revolutions. The pioneers of irreligious philosophical movements are the Jews. Because they are a nation that is fond of life and afraid of death, they have been punished with humiliation and misery.

Fatih Sultan Mehmed was martyred by poisoning Yakup Pasha, the chief doctor of the palace (who was originally a Venetian Jewish convert). Moreover, in those years, the Jews did not have the most feared power. The Ottoman state despised the Jews and the end of the Ottoman Empire was at their hands.

Let me also state that I am an enemy of Zionism, but I am not an enemy of the Jews. I do not approve of the outrage of the Turks who attacked the historical synagogue in Istanbul in order to protest Israel. This is not the order of Islam. Also, the Jewish communities in Istanbul have nothing to do with the issue. The historical synagogue has nothing to do with the issue. Jewish businessmen are said to have allocated a certain amount of money to Israel. I don't know if this is true. If they are giving financial support to Israel, it is likely that Israel is extorting that money from them. This may be the only crime of the Jews in Istanbul. But it is a matter of international law.

Let's finish the Jewish issue by quoting from my book "The Return of Jesus".

Badiuzzaman interprets some verses in the Quran related to the Jews, and he mentions the characteristics of the Jewish nation and their harmful actions to the social life of humanity.

*And they were covered by humiliation and misery.*

One fine point about this verse

> The Jewish nation has always been excessive in its love of life and this world, and has therefore deserved the blows of abasement and misery it has received every century. However, in the Palestine question it is not love of life and this world, but a significant sort of national and religious feeling because Palestine is where the prophets of the Children of Israel are buried, and the prophets belonged to their nation. In consequence they have received no swift blows. A small group could never otherwise have held out in the midst of the vast Arab lands; it would quickly have been humiliated.

BADIUZZAMAN STATES that the Jewish nation is notorious for its intense greed and love of the world. Because of that, they are in poverty. Then why most of the Jews are rich? Because; those Jews who are wealthy gain illicit profit. Moreover; even the rich among them live in a lowly manner. There are also rich people who gain licit profit among them surely. But we mention evil ones. He states this fact as follows:

> Also, among the nations of the world there is none that pursues sustenance more than the Jewish nation, which is notorious for its intense greed. But they have suffered more than any from poor livelihoods amid degradation and poverty. Even the rich among them live in lowly fashion. In any event, the possessions they have acquired by such illicit means as usury do not comprise licit sustenance that it might refute our discussion here.

> *They slaughtered your sons and let your women-folk live.*

> With an event in the time of a Pharaoh, the slaughtering of the sons of the Children of Israel and the sparing of their women and daughters, it mentions the numerous massacres which the Jewish nation has suffered every age, and the role their women and girls have played in dissolute human life.

> And you will indeed find them, of all people, most greedy of life. And you see many of them racing each other in sin and rancour, and their eating of things forbidden. Evil indeed are the things they do. But they ever strive to do mischief on earth. And God

loves not those who do mischief. And We gave clear warning to the Children of Israel in the Book, that twice they would do mischief on the earth. And do no evil nor mischief on the earth.

These two statements of the Qur'an directed at the Jews, comprise the two fearsome general rules, that that nation hatches plots in human social life with their trickery, which shake human society. They say that just as it was that nation which made labour contest with capital; and through usury and compounded interest, made the poor clash with the rich, and caused the banks to be founded, and amassed wealth through wiles and fraud; so it was again that nation who, in order to take their revenge on the victors and governments under which they always suffered deprivation and oppression, were involved in every sort of corrupting covert organization and had a finger in every sort of revolution.

And, for example:

*Then seek ye for death*

That is, "If what you say is true, seek death, but you won't seek it!" Thus, through a minor incident in a small gathering in the presence of the Prophet (PBUH), it points out that the Jewish nation, which is most famous among the nations of mankind for its greed for life and fear of death, will not, according to its tongue of disposition, seek death till Doomsday, and will not give up its greed for life.

And, for example:

*Thus they were stamped with humiliation and indigence.*

With this, it describes generally that nation's future destiny. It is because of these fearsome rules governing the destiny and character of this nation that the Qur'an acts so severely against them. It deals them awesomely punishing slaps. From these examples draw analogies with the other stories and passages about Moses (Peace be upon him) and the Children of Israel. Now, there are very many flashes of miraculousness like the flash in this Fourth Glow behind the simple words and specific subjects of the Qur'an. A hint is enough for the wise.

THE QURAN USES THE most violent expressions for the Jewish disbelievers. For they have gone too far in corruption and oppression. The Jews did not believe in Prophet Muhammad (PBUH) because of their jealousy. Even though they had seen the qualities of Him in the Torah. Because of the fact that they were expecting the last prophet to be of the Jewish nation. They killed the Jewish prophets who were among them, though. But still, there are those who are good people and even prefer the Islam religion in this community. These provisions set the general framework. So we cannot bear enmity toward a community without exception. A real Muslim cannot be an anti-Semitist. This is not what the Quran wants from us. However, every Muslim must be against Zionism. The Zionists do not represent the Jews. They are persecuting the Jews as well. The fact that Islam's invitation to the Jews is valid until the Day of Judgment shows that Islam does not exclude the Jews. The door of Islam is wide open even to the most ferocious Zionist Jews.

DESTINY HAS ASSIGNED two nations to Islam. Arab and Turkish nation.

In eternal knowledge, the Qur'an is determined in Arabic. Arabic was the supreme rhetorical language. And it was a language with a vocabulary that could express sublime truths and abstract concepts in the most effective way. It was a stable language that did not change in terms of words and meaning. Allah had prepared the Arabic language according to the Qur'an.

Destiny made the Arab nation compete in literature, eloquence, poetry, and wise speech thousands of years before the revelation of the Qur'an. This was the centuries-old training for the Arabic language to acquire a richness that would encompass divine will. Because there is no time in divine knowledge. Eternal knowledge has all the times that we call the past and the future.

The Arab people fought the superpowers of the time with great self-sacrifice, sincerity, and submission. They sacrificed their property, their lives, and everything they had for the sake of Islam. They fought heroically when the threats and dangers were the greatest. They were not after fame, mounts, and worldly goods or comfort. Their only goal was Islam and the Qur'an. In this way, they played an important role in the establishment of Islam. Destiny had tasked the Arab nation with the establishment of Islam.

Destiny had chosen another nation for another mission. The Turkish nation was also subjected to different training. This training was war and fight. Attila traveled from Central Asia to Rome on horseback. China suffered so much from the Turkish nation that it built the Great Wall of China, a length of thousands of kilometers. Destiny's plan has brought the Turkish nation into jihad training. Before Islam, the Turks, who constantly fought with the desire for domination and because I would be the head, continued to use their energy to make the religion of Allah prevail when they chose Islam.

The army of the Abbasids consisted of Turks. During the Abbasid period, the Turks took over the flag of jihad from the Arabs and carried out the task of jihad alone for 1000 years. As soon as the Turks converted to Islam, they undertook the duty of jihad, which was obligatory on Muslims.

Meanwhile, Turk is also a negative term as well as a positive term. These terrifying Turks mentioned in hadith sources should not be confused with Muslim Turks. Some Turks are plunderer and murderous tribes that have done great harm to humanity, civilization, and Islam. In certain periods of history, these Turks destroyed all the gain of civilization. Some scholars have said that Yajuj and Majuj, one of the portents of the apocalypse, will emerge from these Turkish tribes. Badiuzzaman is one of those scholars. After quoting Badiuzzaman we will continue with the subject of positive Turks. Badiuzzaman said the following about Gog and Magog (Yajuj and Majuj):

"The events involving Gog and Magog are mentioned concisely in the Qur'an, and there are some details of them in narrations. Those details are not firmly established like the concise but incontrovertible matters of the Qur'an, and may be considered allegorical. They require interpretation. Indeed, they need to be interpreted, for the narrators' interpretations have been mixed in with them.

Yes, *None knows the Unseen save God*, one interpretation is this: it is an allusion and indication that just as the Manchurian and Mongol tribes, which in the heavenly tongue of the Qur'an are called "Gog and Magog" together with some other tribes, several times overturned Asia and Europe; so will they again cause chaos in the world in the future. In fact even now some of them are famous anarchists, and anarchy is born of communism.

Yes, socialism sprang up in the French Revolution from the seed of libertarianism. Then since socialism destroyed certain sacred matters, the ideas it inculcated turned into bolshevism. And because bolshevism corrupted even more sacred moral and human values, and those of the human heart, of course the seeds it sowed will produce anarchy, which recognizes no restrictions whatsoever and has respect for nothing. For if respect and compassion quit the human heart, those with such hearts become exceedingly cruel beasts and can no longer be governed through politics. Just the place for the idea of anarchy will be those oppressed, numerous raiding tribes, which are backward in respect of both civilization and government. The people who fit those conditions are the Manchurian, Mongol, and some of the Kirghiz tribes, who caused the building of the Great Wall of China, which is forty-days' distance in length and is one of the seven wonders of the world. Expounding the Qur'an's concise statements about them, Muhammad (Peace and blessings be upon him) predicted their appearance miraculously and precisely.

Just as at the Divine command, Jesus (Peace be upon him) abrogated some of the burdensome ordinances of the Mosaic Law, making lawful some things agreeable to the appetites like wine, so too at the command of Satan and due to his temptations, the Great Dajjal will abrogate the injunctions of the Christian Law, and destroying the bonds in accordance with which the life of Christian society is administered, he will prepare the ground for anarchy and Gog and Magog. Similarly, the Sufyan, the Islamic Dajjal, due to the devices of Satan and the evil-commanding soul, will try to abrogate some of the eternal injunctions of the Shari'a of Muhammad (PBUH), and destroying the material and spiritual bonds of human life, and leaving headstrong, drunken, giddy souls without restriction, he will unfasten the luminous chains of respect and compassion. By giving people a freedom which is pure despotism so they fall on one another in a swamp of putrid lust, he will open up the way to a terrible anarchy. There will then be no way those people can be kept under control other than by the most repressive despotism."

BEFORE MEETING ISLAM, every nation had idol worship in its past. However, no archaeologist has found a single item in the form of an idol belonging to the Turkish nation before Islam.

Exceptions don't break the rule. There is no such thing as a Christian Turk. Islam and the Turkish nation are an inseparable duo. Turks who left Islam or choose Christinaity have left their Turkish identity. Turks can preserve their Turkish identity with Islam. However, this is not the case for other nations. Among the Arabs, there are those who protect Arabism outside of religion. However, Christian Turks are not called Turks. Although Hungarians and Bulgarians are Turks, they lost their Turkish identity because they chose Christianity.

IT WAS NECESSARY TO dissuade the Turks from their duty of being the leader of the Islamic world and duty of jihad. The Turks had to withdraw into their shells and give up on the cause of Islam.

In the last years of the nineteenth century, in the British Parliament, Minister of Colonies Gladstone showed the Qur'an in his hand and said: "As long as this book remains in the hands of the Muslims, we cannot really dominate them. Either we have to abolish the Qur'an or we should alienate them from the Qur'an."

The Ottoman Empire collapsed and the Republic of Turkey was recognized by the Treaty of Lausanne. Lord Curzon, the head of the British Executive Committee, recognized the independence of the Turks on the following condition: "If Turkey dissolves its Islamic relevance and its role of representing Islam, it will be united with us. And we'll give them what they want."

This condition was accepted by the new Ankara administration. Thereupon, an agreement was signed (1923). In the British House of Commons rose objections, "Why did you recognize the independence of the Turks?" Lord Curzon replied: "The Turks from now on will not be able to regain their former saturation and zeal. Because we have killed them on the spiritual and soul fronts. Because the decision made by Mustafa Kemal and Ismet is the decision to kill the Turkish nation in terms of religion."

Thus, the secular Turkish Republic was established. The British only wanted the abolition of the caliphate. However, the Ankara government voluntarily put pressure on the Muslims. Adhans were recited in Turkish. Saying "Allah" was forbidden. People were forced to wear a fedora hats. Those who did not wear hats were executed....

Adnan Menderes, the prime minister who restored the adhan to its original Arabic, was executed (1961).

Subsequent governments continued to remove Islamic restrictions gradually.

SO WHERE WILL THIS trend lead?

Hazrat Muhyiddin Arabi answers our question: "After the Ottoman Empire, there will be a pause for 100 years. Then the state to be established will have 10 Ottoman forces."

After 2023, the Republic of Turkey will begin to take on a new character. It will become an unstoppable force in the 2030s. Of course, this power will be in the military, political and economic fields. Otherwise, it will not be able to catch up with the Ottomans in terms of social, cultural, and artistic aspects.

Today's Turkey is not fully living Islam. Crimes such as extortion, murder, and fraud are quite commonplace. Very few people are religious. People began to blindly imitate the west and admire western countries in the last century of the Ottoman Empire. Allah shook Turkey with the First World War. He punished the Turks at the hand of the western countries. Later, He penetrated a weak enemy like the Greeks into Anatolia. Then the people of Anatolia got rid of the Greeks, but they could not escape the punishment. It is still crushed under the pressure of the secular regime.

I would like to say a few words to avoid misunderstandings. My use of the term "weak enemy" to Greece was never intended to humiliate the Greek nation. On the contrary, it was to point out the situation the Ottomans had fallen into. In fact, it was the Ottoman Empire that was weak. It was meant to express the bitter situation of a nation (Muslim Turks) that had been a superpower for 1000 years (approximately) and ruled three continents. Otherwise, we lived together with Greek and Armenian nations in Anatolia for centuries. During the Ottoman period, non-Muslim nations (especially Istanbul) added cultural richness to the country... The architects of most of the great historical buildings in Turkey were Greeks and Armenians (including some mosques). In this respect, we love the Armenian and Greek nations. The Ottomans gave the title of the loyal nation to the Armenians living in the Anatolian lands.

For a century, Turks have been governed by the constitution of western countries, which they have admired. And after every incident that affects the public conscience, "where is the justice?" is being shouted. Let me tell you where the justice is. Justice is in the constitution of the Qur'an. It is only foolishness for Islamic states to seek help from the constitution created with the short mind of man.

Greece does not want the war of its own will, it is guided by the global mind. The global mind wants to start some wars in the world. One of these wars is the Turkey-Greece war. Turkey is not playing this trick and it is trying its best not to go to war with Greece.

Greece wants to draw Turkey into the war by relying on some western states. Turkey is trying to solve the problems between the two states through diplomacy. I won't go into details as it's a political issue.

I have to say this because it is a reality. Turkey does not want war. However, when war is inevitable, no power can prevent the Turkish nation. It seems that Greece does not realize how dangerous a game it is playing. The states behind it can neither protect nor save Greece. I hope that the disputes between the two countries will be resolved through diplomatic means.

If Greece does not give up on this dangerous stubbornness, Turkey will easily seize the islands armed by Greece. At this point, if Greece accepts defeat and withdraws, a major war will be averted. However, if Greece wants to take the war forward by relying on the support of the states behind it, they will meet the real power of the Turkish army. Turkish Defense Industry President İsmail Demir: "Let them think that the balance of power has changed. We don't want it, but when the power has to be shown on the field, they will see who has the power!"

If a war broke out between Turkey and Greece today, who would win?

If we respond to the circle of causes, that is, according to the principles of creation in the universe, Greece will suffer a great defeat. No matter how many weapons, fighter jets and warships it buys from which country, it has no chance against the current Turkish army.

Turkey has made incredible breakthroughs in war technology. It is able to defeat its enemies without firing a single bullet. The Turkish army is among the best in the world in electronic warfare technology. This is a completely separate topic. Also, I won't open the issue since it's national security. I'm just going to cite an incident that happened. In the past years, a French frigate is coming to the region in the eastern Mediterranean, which Turkey has declared a navtex. And it is forced to flee the area. According to the reports in the French and UAE media, the French frigate in the region wants to call for help to the Greek authorities in a radio conversation by saying: "All the digital displays of our ship are locked. Our navigation is not working. Our weapon systems have fallen to the 'off' position. Hundreds of unidentified objects are flying over us. We can't figure out what they are. It locked down our entire system. The ship's entire digital system is out of our control. Send us a guide."

However, it turns out that the French ship's request for help could not reach the Greek Coastal Command. Probably because Turkey blocked it. When the French frigate realizes that no help will come, it is forced to flee the area. After this event, the tracking and observation ship of the USA called the "floating base", comes to Crete with the "emergency code". The USA explains that its intention is to observe the activities in the region and to figure out what kind of system Turkey is using.

On the other hand, if divine punishment comes to Turkey, Greece enters the Anatolian lands. Turkey's military power is of no use. God neutralizes that power for various reasons. This is not a very remote possibility. Because the Turkish nation has gone astray and it is possible that they will suffer divine punishment. Allah is not pleased with the current Turkish people.

That is, victory and defeat are from Allah. If God wants to punish the Turkish nation, He will pave the way for Greece and other states that are allies against Turkey. The Turkish nation will have to fight for 5-10 years. Just like at the beginning of the 20th century.

Turkey is not punished by divine punishment for some reasons. But as long as the people of Anatolia go beyond the limit, they may be exposed to disasters from the earth and sky.

The main reasons that protect Anatolia from earthly and heavenly troubles are as follows:

Anatolia is the castle of ahlussunnah wal jamaah.

The Turkish nation has served Islam for 1000 years. Grandchildren are not punished for the sake of their ancestors.

The people of Anatolia will once again be the leader of the Islamic world. And the Turkish army will serve Islam again. They are not punished as a reward for their future service.

Even though Turkey is currently governed by a secular system, it is still the center of the Islamic world. The caliphate ship sank here and will rise again from here.

The troubles I'm talking about are long-term and big troubles. Otherwise, disasters such as earthquakes and floods occur as a divine punishment/warning in Turkey. Allah protects Anatolia from greater disasters.

*Say: "He hath power to send calamities on you, from above and below, or to cover you with confusion in party strife, giving you a taste of mutual vengeance - each from the other." See how We explain the signs by various (symbols); that they may understand. (Surah Al-An'am, Verse 65)*

Speaking of Anatolia, there is a special bond between the Anatolian lands and the Muslim Turkish nation. When the civil war broke out in Syria, those fleeing the war immigrated to Turkey. Anatolian lands are a safe harbor. However, in case of war, no one leaves Anatolia. The Muslim Turkish nation sacrifices their lives, but they do not leave Anatolia. In the 20th century, the Ottoman Empire lost all its lands except Anatolian lands. When Anatolian lands were in question, they fought all-out and did not surrender Anatolia. Sultan Alparslan, the glorious commander who defeated the Byzantine army in Manzikert (26 August 1071) and made Anatolia a homeland for the Turks, said: I captured you such a homeland; will be yours forever.

We have also expressed one of the reasons why Anatolia is under the grace of Allah. Anatolia is the last refuge of Muslims. When the threat reaches Anatolia, God's grace and help come into play. Just like the failed coup attempt on July 15, 2016. By the grace of God, the coup failed. The traitors in the Turkish army have been exposed. In this way, Allah strengthened the Turkish army. The enemy made a plan, but there was another plan at work. Destiny's plan... Destiny's plan operated to make the Turkish army ready for conquests.

# Naval Battle of Preveza



*Venice, Papal States, Genoa, Spain, Mantua, Malta, Portugal against the Ottoman Empire*

"WHEN TALUT SET FORTH with the armies, he said: "Allah will test you at the stream: if any drinks of its water, He goes not with my army: Only those who taste not of it go with me: A mere sip out of the hand is excused." but they all drank of it, except a few. When they crossed the river,- He and the faithful ones with him,- they said: "This day We cannot cope with Goliath and his forces." but those who were convinced that they must meet Allah, said: "How oft, by Allah's will, Hath a small force vanquished a big one? Allah is with those who steadfastly persevere." (Surah Al-Baqarah, 2:249)

THE BATTLE OF PREVEZA was fought between the Ottoman navy and the allied Crusader navy on September 28, 1538. This legendary war is of great importance in terms of determining Ottoman dominance in the Mediterranean. When evaluated in terms of causes or usual laws of the universe, it was expected that the Ottomans would definitely lose this war. However, the Ottomans gained an overwhelming advantage against the crusaders.

The activities of the Ottomans towards the Venetian islands and lands in the Aegean and Adriatic caused an alliance to be made in February 1538, under the leadership of Pope Paolo III, in order to win the struggle of the Christian states for dominance in the seas and to drive the Ottomans away from the Mediterranean. Andrea Doria, known as Europe's greatest sailor, was appointed to the head of the navy.

Venice, Portugal, Malta, and Genoa also joined the alliance between Spain, the papacy, and Austria. Thus, a sizeable Christian navy was created under the command of Andrea Doria. The Allied navy began to assemble in Corfu in March 1538. With the completion of the assembly, the navy besieged the Preveza Fortress at the northern entrance of Narda Bay on September 7, 1538. Hearing this, Barbarossa Hayreddin Pasha sent a volunteer fleet of twenty ships under the command of Turgut Reis as a pioneer. Turgut Reis encountered an enemy fleet of forty ships in the waters of Zenta. He reported the situation to Barbarossa, who was in Modon then. An Allied fleet in Zenta also went to Preveza and informed Andrea Doria about the Ottoman fleet. Thereupon, the Allied fleet left Preveza and withdrew to Corfu. Barbarossa Hayreddin Pasha, on the other hand, plundered the island of Kefalonia in return for the destruction of the Preveza Castle. After he came to Preveza Castle on September 24, 1538, and repaired it, he began to stand by in the bay. The next day, the Allied fleet anchored again off Preveza. The presence of the Allied navy was different, but Spain and Portugal had eighty galleons. Venice had ten galleons and seventy galleys. Papacy owned thirty-six galleys, Malta ten. The Genoese had a galleon and fifty-two galleys. The Allied navy consisted of 140 galleons with square sails, 168 galleys and many transport ships, including forty-nine galleons belonging to other states. It also consisted of 60,000 soldiers. On the other hand, there were 122 galley type ships and 12-20,000 soldiers in the navy of Barbarossa.

In total, the allied navy consisted of 608 ships, 2,500 guns, and 60,000 soldiers. On the other hand, there were 122 ships, 366 guns, and between 8 and 20 thousand soldiers in the navy of Barbarossa Hayreddin Pasha. 102 of the navy under the command of Barbarossa belonged to the Ottoman state and 20 of them belonged to volunteer pirates. Although there are different opinions about the numbers, historians agree that the Allied navy was far superior to the Ottoman navy in terms of numbers. And the Allied navy was the largest ever seen.

In the war council convened by Barbarossa, different views emerged on how to act due to the power imbalance. The navy was advised to stay in Narda bay. Sinan Reis and his supporters recommended that the Preveza Castle be protected by landing soldiers and placing them on the shores opposite the allied navy. Barbarossa Hayreddin Pasha opposed this. Andrea Doria made three attacks on 23, 24, and 25 September to besiege Barbarossa in the bay. However, the Ottoman guards repulsed them. Because the entrance to the bay was shallow, galleons in the Allied fleet could not enter. However, because the entry was closed, the front of the Ottoman navy was also cut off.

Although there was an attack from the allied navy on September 25, 1538, the Ottoman ships under the command of Turgut Reis, Murad Aga, and Mehmed Reis took action and came out of the bay and repelled this attack. On Friday, September 27, Barbarossa opened out from the bay with the navy and after 6 miles, all galleys started the war by firing three cannons. When Andrea Doria, put his navy in a dangerous position with a wrong maneuver, Barbarossa sent a fleet of forty ships to split the allied navy into two, and Andrea Doria, seeing this, ordered his navy to retreat towards Corfu. In the face of this situation, Barbarossa anchored his fleet in front of Preveza, outside the Narda Gulf, due to the darkening of the air.

On September 28, Andrea Doria came back to fight in accordance with the decision of the war council he convened. To meet them, the Ottoman navy advanced in line toward the allied navy. Barbarossa arranged his navy in a crescent shape. Barbarossa was in the center, Salih Reis on the right wing, Seydi Ali Reis on the left wing, and Turgut Reis with his fleet of volunteer chiefs behind this line. In the Allied navy, apart from Andrea Doria, who commanded the Spanish imperial navy, Vicenzo Capello was commanding the Venetian navy and Marco Grimani was commanding the papal navy.

In front of the first line of the allied navy, which was lined up in a broadside order and in three ranks, was the great Venetian galleon and the galleons that would serve as trenches. Galleys were lined up in the second row and other small ships in the third row. Andrea Doria was in charge of the second-row galleys. According to this order, when the two fleets met off Preveza, a strong southerly wind from Africa was blowing. This wind was in favor of the allied navy and against the Ottoman galleys. Andrea Doria, taking advantage of the wind, launched a counterattack. He was sure that the Ottomans would lose the war. Heavy galleons traveling rapidly with the wind could crush the Pasha's light galleys. It seemed impossible for the Ottomans to stop the Allied navy with big sails, which came upon them like a floating fortress. Taking this strong wind behind him, Andrea Doria's 150 galleys in the forward line rushed forward, too. If the wind continued to blow like this, they would crush the Ottoman navy. Struggling against the wind, Barbarossa gave the order to shoot the high-range Turkish artillery after raising the sails. He was trying not to let the Crusader fleets approach. Relying on the wind, Andrea Doria was confident of victory. Barbarossa, who knew the winds of the Mediterranean well, was waiting for the wind to stop for the movement.

Barbarossa orders all soldiers to write these two verses from the Qur'an on a piece of paper and leave them into the sea from both sides of the ships in order to strengthen his own soldier's spirituality. "If it be His Will He can still the Wind: then would they become motionless on the back of the (ocean). Verily in this are Signs for everyone who patiently perseveres and is grateful. (Surah Ash-Shura, Verse 33)" "O ye who believe! Remember the Grace of Allah, (bestowed) on you, when there came down on you hosts (to overwhelm you): But We sent against them a hurricane and forces that ye saw not: but Allah sees (clearly) all that ye do. (Surah Al-Ahzab, Verse 9)"

Finally, the wind stopped. This time, the galleons in the allied navy remained motionless. Andrea Doria launched a massive cannon fire from the galleons ahead. However, due to the short range of the galleon cannons, all the cannonballs fell into the sea. Since the Ottoman galleys had both oars and sails, this time the advantage fell into the hands of the Pasha. When the Pasha counterattacked, the galleons were targeted and hit first, thanks to the long gun range of the Ottoman galleys. After the effect of the great galleons was broken, Hayreddin Pasha went on the offensive to break through the galleons of the crusaders and attack their galleys from the front in order to bring the war to a definite conclusion. Ottoman galleys, which had fast maneuverability, quickly passed through the galleons and began to hit the crusader galleys. The Allies embarked on an operation to encircle the Ottoman fleet with the second row of galleys. However, they were repelled by heavy artillery and Turgut Reis' encircling tactic. While Andrea Doria wanted to leave the ships of Barbarossa between two fires, he was caught between two fires. Andrea Doria wanted to try a few more times with the plan to put the Ottoman fleet under fire. But each time he failed because of Barbarossa's quick maneuvers. Most of the galleons at the forefront of the allied fleet were destroyed in these attacks. Barbarossa, who gave the order to attack to break through the Allied fleet, divided the first row into two and attacked the galleys under the command of Andrea Doria. Trying to surround the Turkish navy, Andrea Doria's ships were surrounded by Barbarossa each time. Turgut Reis, who took the west wind behind him, surrounded the crusaders from behind with his own fleet. The Crusader fleet was under siege from all sides. Crusader ships, unable to maneuver and shoot, crashed and merged with each other. The war order of the Crusader ships was broken and they panicked. Faced with the danger of being destroyed, Andrea Doria decided to withdraw. Doria understood that he had lost the war, and he did not want to suffer any more casualties. Taking advantage of the dark, Andrea Doria began to retreat, ordering the ships to put out their light.

At the end of the battle, the losses of both sides were as follows:

The largest flagship of Venice has been captured by the Turks. 128 ships belonging to the Crusaders were sunk and 36 ships were captured by the Turkish navy. 3000 soldiers were captured.

Barbarossa had no ship loss. There were 400 martyrs and 800 wounded in his navy.

Besides Barbarossa's tactic, the galleys in the navy impacted the victory of the Battle of Preveza. Small and fast galleys, capable of navigating shallow waters, had defeated the large galleons of the crusaders. This victory led to the preference for galley-type ships for a long time in the Ottoman navy.

# The Battle of Gallipoli

---

*Çanakkale is impassable!*

*Because the Turks did not even have gunpowder to shoot.*

*We saw the forces descending from the sky there.*

*__________ British Commander Hamilton*

The Battle of Gallipoli (the battle of Çanakkale) is the naval and land battles between the Ottoman Empire and the Entente Powers on the Gallipoli Peninsula between 1915-1916 during the First World War. On this front, the Ottoman state and Germany fought together. The Entente Powers could not pass the Dardanelles and the Ottomans won the war with a decisive victory.

The Entente Powers wanted to pass the Dardanelles in order to capture Istanbul, defeat the Ottomans, throw the Ottomans out of the war and provide ammunition, soldiers and supplies to tsarist Russia.

The Ottomans fought on many fronts in the First World War and lost the war on all fronts. The only front it won was the Çanakkale front. Although the Ottomans lost on all other fronts, Allah helped the Turks on the Çanakkale front. Because this front was gate to Anatolia, the eternal home of the Muslim Turkish nation...

Allah did not allow the British Empire and France to cross the Dardanelles. He did not want the Entente Powers to capture Istanbul, the capital of the caliphate, with a sword victory. God would give the British a table victory at the end of the war.

The British, who could not pass the Çanakkale, would beat the Turks at the table (Treaty of Lausanne,1923). The caliphate would be abolished and a secular state would be established. If the British had invaded Anatolia, they would not have been able to abolish the caliphate.

Destiny plan operates far beyond our understanding. According to the destiny plan, the Caliphate would abandon the Muslims anyway. The Muslims were no longer worthy of the caliphate and did not like the caliphate. They wanted to be governed by the laws of the West.

Gallipoli is also a war with a high moral value, which has rare memories in the history of world war. Turkish soldiers and Anzac troops met while fighting each other and became friends. Some Anzacs shared emotional memories of the war. I will not talk about those memories in this book. I mentioned this to draw attention to the fact that Gallipoli is such a war that it has memories, friendships and experiences that are remembered years later.

Let's move on to our subject, enough for an introduction.

The Battle of Gallipoli is a topic in itself. I will not go into details such as the process of the war, the losses, the comparison of the parties in terms of soldiers, equipment, weapons, ships, planes, etc.

Çanakkale, the place where the reasons are exhausted, is a holy place where the grace and help of Allah descends upon the Muslims. I'm going to narrate some incredible events that cannot be explained by the laws of physics.

# Cevat Pasha's Dream

The commander of the Çanakkale fortified area, Cevat Pasha, had fallen into a light sleep because of extreme tiredness, while he was saddened in the face of the bombardments of the enemy navies stationed in the Bosphorus. He heard a voice in his dream:

"O Cevat! You respect and honor the supreme word of Allah. For this reason, I give you good news with the help of Allah Almighty. Take a look over that sea!"

Looking towards the sea, Cevat Pasha sees the sparkling letters "kāf" and "wāw" (و and ك) adorned with flowers among the waves. Cevat Pasha, who wakes up with excitement, cannot make sense of the dream.

The next day, Cevat Pasha heard the voice in his dream while he was at a grave (Tomb of the great saint Ahmed Cahidi Sultan):

"O Cevat! Lay the 26 mines in the warehouses into the sea!"

He got excited. He was faced with a spiritual enigma. While thinking about how to solve this, he soon came across a glowing faced person who was looking at him. That person approached Pasha, holds his arm, and asked if he had a problem. Pasha also told what had happened. The glowing-faced man answers:

"The light is the sign of victory. In the abjad reckoning, the letter "kāf" indicates 20, and "wāw" indicates the number 6 and makes 26..."

After these words, that glowing-faced person (Ahmed Cahidi Sultan) disappeared from sight. (A saint who has passed away appears to Cevat Pasha, who is at his grave. Cevat Pasha came to the tomb of this blessed person as follows. He goes out to inspect some batteries to reinforce them. While getting on the steamboat from Kilitbahir, he remembers his daughter Bedile Hanım, who died of tuberculosis seven years ago. His daughter's grave is in the *hazire* of the tomb of Ahmed Cahidi Sultan, a friend of Allah... When he comes to his grave, he hears the voice in his dream again. *Hazire* is a burial area reserved for special people, especially in mosques or Sufi lodges.)

Cevat Pasha immediately calls Nazmi Bey to find out how many mines are in the warehouses.

Nazmi Bey says that they have 26 mines made by a Turkish master. He adds: "The German technicians did not want us to lay these." There were 377 mines in the Bosphorus all German-made."

Cevat Pasha immediately gave an order for the aforementioned mines to be laid. The mines were placed in the water at midnight under the command of Captain Hakki Bey with the Nusret Mine Ship. Captain Hakki Bey died of a heart attack after completing his duty.

The next day, when the enemy battleships entered the Bosphorus, the mines began to perform their duties. Some important battleships of the enemy navy were buried in the waters of the Bosphorus with these mines. Thus, the attack of the enemy was defeated.

THESE 26 MINES LAID by Nusret are the most important turning point of the war. Nusret performed a very important task that will pass not only to Turkish history, but also to world history. If Nusret had not laid those mines that day, land battles would probably not have happened, the defenses on both sides of the fortified area would have fallen and the British would have been able to reach the target they had set for themselves (Istanbul).

I WILL NOT GO INTO technical details and how this mine mission is carried out. Our topic is divine help and unexplained mysteries. Apart from Cevat Pasha's dream, another unexplained mysterious event is reported:

Considering the great danger, mines were laid and the return journey had begun. The danger was not over yet. The mines could have exploded. In addition, the patrol ships of the Allied Powers were on Nusret's return route. A silhouette appeared close to Nusret. Most likely, the enemy was back on patrol. If It turned on the searchlights to scan the sea, it would all be over. The sea was calm, the air was pitch dark. The feared thing happened to them and the searchlights of the enemy ship were turned on. The light, which broke through the darkness and scanning the sea, shores and waves, was coming towards them. Seconds before they were caught in the light waves, a searchlight suddenly on the Turkish coast caught the enemy ship in a few seconds. The two searchlights came face to face. An intense whiteness covered the area. The enemy ship was trying hard to get rid of the Turkish searchlight, but failed. The Nusret ship was saved from an absolute defeat thanks to this intense light war. The mysterious and unexplained incident here was that the Turkish searchlight was out of order. It worked again without any repairs.

# Corporal Seyit



*A Christian commander asks Fatih Sultan Mehmet Khan:*

*"How do you come out victorious in every battle? Whatever we did, no matter what we tried, we couldn't defeat you."*

*Fatih Sultan Mehmet Khan answers: "Why are we not defeated? Because we also have an army in the sky!"*

Corporal Seyit Ali played a very important role in winning the Dardanelles War. He single-handedly lifted the 276-pound cannonball and placed it in the barrel.

Corporal Seyit was an artilleryman in the Dardanelles Front. On March 18, 1915, the Allied fleet attacked to pass through the Dardanelles. Meanwhile, he was in charge of the Rumeli Mecidiye Bastion. The intense counterfire of the Turkish artillery and the mines previously laid by the Nusret minelayer repulsed this attack. Due to intense shooting, the bullet lifting crane of the cannon in the bastion was broken. Thereupon, Corporal Seyit carried the 276 kilograms of cannonballs on his back and placed them in the artillery carriage.

The Rumeli Mecidiye Bastion was almost completely destroyed as a result of a terrible enemy attack. Most of the arsenal was blown up, and sixteen artillerymen were martyred. Only a captain, two soldiers, a single cannon with a broken crane survived.

The captain had moved away to report the situation to the surrounding troops. Seyit Ali sighed deeply, looking at the enemy ships. Tears flowed from his eyes. He raised his hands to the Almighty and prayed to Allah to give him strength.

The future of the capital and the Islamic world was in his hands. If the ships passed the Bosphorus, Anatolia would be out of the hands of the Muslims. It was at that moment that the power of faith in Seyit Ali's heart was manifested.

He suddenly cried out, "O Allah!" and, amid the astonishment of his friend, he grasped the 276-kilogram bullet and lifted it.

He did some light damage to Ocean in the first two shots. In his third shot, he badly injured the British battleship Ocean. The projectile hit slightly below the waterline of the ship, causing the ship to tilt instantly. Later, Ocean struck one of the mines laid by the Nusret minelayer. The British battleship Ocean capsized and sank shortly after this wound.

IT IS QUITE POSSIBLE that angels took part in a war with a high spiritual aspect like Çanakkale. There are rumors on this subject, but I will not include (all of) them in this work.

However, angels did not appear to everyone clearly (due to the secret of testing). Besides, it is possible for the spirits of martyrs and saints to be present in Çanakkale. (For example, it is mentioned about the awliya—passed away—who gave water to the wounded Muslim soldiers.) The friends of Allah are discussing important events in islamic world among themselves in the realm of barzakh. Their death differs greatly from the death of the common people... Death manifests differently for everyone...

In Çanakkale, the material power of the Turks was so low that it could not even be compared with the power of the enemy. Until the soldier went from Istanbul to Çanakkale, the boot on his foot was falling apart. Sometimes they had no gunpowder to shoot.

Since spirituality was stronger than matter, matter was under its influence. Therefore, in Çanakkale, the Allied Powers army, which had all kinds of technical equipment and the most advanced war inventory of the time, had to submit to the Turkish army, which was much weaker in terms of numbers and weapons but was extremely strong in terms of faith and spirituality. Because the Turkish soldiers compensated for the lack of weapons with the power of faith.

THE FOLLOWING CONFESSION of the British army commander, General Hamilton, shows this fact:

"The moral power, not the material power of the Turks, defeated us. Because they didn't even have gunpowder to shoot. But we witnessed the forces that came down from the sky and helped them!"

AND CHURCHILL WAS PRESSED: "How could you not beat the Turks despite all this technology?" He replied:

"Don't you understand, we fought with God in Çanakkale, not the Turks."

CHURCHILL PROPOSED using chemical gas in the House of Lords after the war was prolonged and the British could not get any results. When he was reminded that this was a crime against humanity and did not fit into the morality of war, he convinced the parliamentarians by saying that Turks were not human beings; they were animals/ barbarians. (Winston Churchill's notes during the First World War and the letter of persuasion he wrote to the Royal Air Force, which was opposed to him, show that he wanted to use poison gas in Çanakkale. Churchill is thought to support Gladstone's view that "Turks are civilization-destroying barbarians between ape and man".) Chemical gas was shipped to Çanakkale in barrels from England. Since the season was summer, the wind blew from the sea toward the land. According to the calculations of the British, the lids of the barrels at sea will be opened and the Turkish soldiers engaged in defensive warfare on land will be poisoned. However, divine help overturns their cheating. The wind changed direction and continued to blow from land to sea until the end of the war. The British could not achieve these goals thanks to Allah's grace to the Turks.

In an interview with a Çanakkale veteran, he is asked whether he has seen green turbans (he was probably asked if he had seen angels too, since the angels seen in war were wearing green turbans). The veteran answers: "No, we did not see it. There were only green birds. They would wander among the fire. Then they would land on the olive trees. Those olive trees were broken with bullets, cannonballs, and destroyed. Those green birds used to land there. The bullet did not touch them."

THE COMMANDERS DID not allow the soldiers who wanted to perform the Eid prayer. Because praying in groups would be a unique opportunity for the enemy. Although the weather was clear on the day of Arafa, clouds had descended on the trenches on the morning of the feast. So much so that it was impossible for the enemy to see the Turkish soldiers. Turks performed the Eid prayer. Then they started to say the eid takbirs with ecstasy. The sound of takbir, which was fluctuating in unison, could be heard from the enemy trenches. At this time, confusion arose in the ranks of the enemy. Gunshots were heard. It turns out that the British had deceived them when they were recruiting soldiers from Muslim colonial countries. They said, "Your caliph has been kidnapped by the Germans. We are going to war with the Germans to save your caliph." The Muslim colonies, who heard the takbir, realized that they were fighting against the Muslims and rebelled against the British in their trenches. The British, on the other hand, shot some of these soldiers and sent some of them to the rear.

SOME WANTED TO THANK a commander. The commander didn't like it at all. He said:

"We have witnessed such incidents here that they are only the protection of Allah. It is nothing else. There have been such events that neither mind nor science can call anything. One day, the enemy would make a landing. There was intense bombardment before the landing. They started bombing a location. They fired hundreds of thousands of bullets. There is no stone left on the stone, there is no air left to smell. It is not possible for our soldiers in our trench line to survive. We thought our soldiers were martyred and buried under the ground. The enemy also came to the same conclusion and started to landing. When it was time, the cry of 'Allah, Allah!' broke out. The whole trench line went up to attack. It's as if the angels had their wings stretched out and hid them. The enemy was stunned by this marvel. Both the mind and science were embarrassed here."

LIEUTENANT COLONEL Sefik Bey and the Turkish soldiers with him are trying to cross the plain for a long period of about an hour. Although the soldiers advance in front of the navy, balloons, and planes, they are not under fire. The navy's fire begins after crossing the plain. They are pounding the plain left behind by the Turks entirely from beginning to end. Turkish soldiers, on the other hand, have no idea which target was hit. Because there is no target on the plain to hit.

It seems that the attack planes do not see the Turkish soldiers advancing to the front. Thanks to the sudden veil drawn over the eyes of the enemy, they are saved from death. Turkish soldiers are getting rid of an absolute defeat with the grace of Allah.

# The Sinai Desert

Yavuz Sultan Selim Khan led an expedition to Egypt with the goal of uniting Islam under a single flag. During this expedition, he crossed the Sinai desert in a short period of thirteen days. Genghis and Timur could not pass it and had to return several times.

There are two rulers in history who crossed the Sinai Desert with their armies. Kambiz, the Shah of Iran, is one. Alexander, King of Macedonia, is the other.

Yavuz Sultan Selim completed this impossible task in thirteen days with no casualties or supply problems. Other rulers attempted to cross the desert by using horse-drawn carriages to shield them from the sun. Yavuz Sultan Selim, on the other hand, led the entire expedition on horseback. Even Napoleon, the great military genius, was unable to complete this task three hundred years after Yavuz, and the French soldiers shot each other, going mad with thirst. Even with the opportunities offered by science and tanks, this desert could be crossed in eleven days during the First World War.

Between Gaza and Egypt, there were three large deserts. One of them was the Sinai Desert. Without crossing these deserts, it was impossible to reach Egypt by land. Because Hulagu Khan and Timur, who had previously considered coming here, were unable to cross these deserts, the Egyptian land was spared their invasion.

The temperature difference between day and night in this unforgiving desert ranged between +50 and -20 degrees.

This sand sea was entered thanks to Yavuz's incredible determination. After a while, Yavuz Sultan Selim dismounted his horse and began to walk in front of his soldiers, humbly bent over.

The military staff was astonished and bewildered. Seeing that the Sultan of the entire world was walking in front of them, the soldiers got off their horses and started walking. Hasan Can, a close friend of Yavuz Selim Han, curiously asks Selim why he got off his horse and walked. Yavuz says:

"Can't you see Hasan, the Messenger of Allah, the pride of the universe (PBUH), is walking before us? How can we be on horseback while that sultan of the realms walks on foot?"

HULAGU KHAN AND TIMUR, by the way, are Turkish, but they are brutal enemies of Islam. It is forbidden to love them, and we do not.

# My Little Infidels

The cannons fired during the siege for the conquest of Istanbul could not find their target. Fatih's hodja, Akshemseddin, investigates the reason for this. (Hazrat Akshemseddin is the spiritual conqueror of Istanbul.) It's found the reason for the delay of the conquest. Jibali Baba, one of the mad awliyas(saints) located within the walls of Istanbul, was spiritually honored by the name of Vedud of the Almighty. He was praying, "My Lord! Protect my little infidels." Thus, the cannons were not effective.

Akshemseddin worked for forty days. He was honored by the name of Vedud. He even surpassed Jibali Baba. Dismissed him from the rank he reached. After that, the cannons started to hit the target. Thus, after a long and tiring siege, Istanbul was conquered.

According to another rumor, Akshemseddin, who is aware of the situation, raises his hand and prays: "O Lord, take my life or Jibali Baba, so that the conquest will be successful!" And with the acceptance of this prayer, on May 28, 1453, one day before the conquest, Jibali Baba passed away. Thus, the conquest takes place.

Awliya, who is in such a temptation, may not be responsible because of the enthusiasm of spiritual drunkenness. But he cannot guide others as he is.

Such saints vanish in the presence and unity of Allah so much that they are too ecstatic to notice the existence. In this state, they lose their reasoning and mental balance. They are not responsible for the things they say and the deeds they do while this situation is victorious.

*I didn't want to use the term 'mad' for a saint. However, I could not find the appropriate word in English. In Turkish, the word denoting 'mad', which is used for people who are devoted to God, who have lost their minds with the love of God, and who are in love with God, is not used negatively. For such people, a unique word is used, which means insanity positively.*

*The other word used in Turkish but not in English is the softened version of the word 'infidel'. Since the word 'Infidel' can mean insulting, another softer word is preferred instead of this word. (Although they don't use either word in the face of non-muslims)The kind-spirited Muslim Turks softened the word 'infidel' so that the Christians would not perceive it as an insult and used the word 'giaour' (non-Muslim, especially Christian, European person) instead. Jibali Baba also uses this soft word. The word that does not mean this insult is still used in Turkish today. However, since the word 'giaour' has no equivalent in English, the word 'infidel' is used in translations In addition, it is not appropriate to call non-Muslims with whom we are in peace or who live among Muslims 'infidel'. Because it is torture. Islamic scholars decide that it is not permissible to call an unbeliever "O infidel", as it would mean insult and hatred.*

# Angels

———

Angel belief is crucial among the pillars of belief because angels are envoys who carry heavenly messages from Allah and disclose them to the prophets. So, believing in revelations and prophets necessitates first believing in the presence of angels who reveal the revelations and prophethood. Not believing in angels means not believing in prophets. That is why believing in Angels comes right after believing in Allah.

The subject of angels is a broad one. We will mostly deal with the aspects related to our subject.

Let's start with those who deny angels because they have not seen them.

*Why cannot we see Angels?*

Lack of sight does not prove absence.

People, who reject the existence of angels say, "we do not see angels; how can we accept something that we do not see?" However, this statement implies several further things besides the rejection of angels. In this world, man's five senses can only see a small number of things.

Our eyes can only see things that are a fifth of a millimeter in size. Can we reject items that are less than a fifth of a millimeter in this situation?

The neurons in our retina layer cannot perceive hundreds or even thousands of lights. We can not see ultraviolet, radar, gamma, and radioactive rays.

The forces of attraction and repulsion are invisible. However, no individual disputes the reality of such forces. All scientists accept as true what they do not observe. Humanity has not yet witnessed someone use the excuse "I cannot see" to contest the existence of gravity, the force of gravity, and the attraction and repelling properties of stars.

Moreover, the mental, imaginative, and memory faculties in our bodies are far more miraculous than the ones that are visible outworld.

It would take a lot of time to attempt to count things we couldn't see. Man cannot possibly observe even a billionth of the cosmos. Can we then reject the remainder?

Because Angels were made from noor (light), their true natures and genuine images are invisible to human sight. Our vision was not designed with the ability to perceive angels. However, because Allah endowed prophets with the capacity to perceive angels, they could see them in their actual forms.

Our inability to see and perceive angels with our five senses does not imply that they do not exist. In the material world, sense organs cannot observe many things. Our ears cannot detect very low and high-pitched noises. We would know the world quite differently if we could see all light waves. We cannot reject the infinite happenings that occur in our world since we do not know the facts of their occurrences.

It is obvious that just because something cannot be seen with the naked eye does not mean it does not exist. There are many things we cannot see, yet we accept their existence through our reasoning, knowledge, experience, and experimentation.

Angels are mentioned in all heavenly religions. Prophets saw them and got revelations from them. Considering that prophets are the most moral and reliable people among humanity, it will be understood how solid proof this is. Specifically, the Qur'an and all divine scriptures mention the presence of angels. All of these occurrences are clear pieces of evidence of angels' existence.

In actuality, each sense in a person unlocks a door to a separate universe; a sense's responsibility is not required of another sense. For example, the eye cannot serve the function of the ear, and the nose cannot serve the function of the nose. Through his eyes, a man cannot taste the fruit, hear the birds, or smell the fragrance of a rose. Sight can not fulfill the tasks of these senses, as well as the activities of the intellect. It is the same as expecting the nose's function from the ear to expect the eye to do the mind's function.

In conclusion, human beings do not reject the existence of things they cannot see; rather, they accept their existence based on a variety of facts and suppositions. He must therefore acknowledge the angels' reality as well. Given the abundance of evidence, accepting it is not at all difficult.

Angels are subtle creatures and can transform into various forms. They do not have the ability to do evil in their nature. They are just programmed to do good deeds.

Angels are Allah's devoted servants. They follow instructions and carry them through. Never do they disobey or act in an unauthorized manner. They are without any sin. Without being ordered, they cannot take action.

They are neither spiritually developing nor decreasing since they lack nafs, rage, and desire. Satan doesn't touch them. Since they do not contend with nafs and devils, they each have a fixed status and a constant rank.

Angels do not eat, drink, sleep, get married, or have children. They are genderless. They can quickly reach even the most remote locations. They can take on whatever shape or form they choose.

Their service itself is their reward. Noor (light) is delightful to them. They like also pleasant odors. Certainly, superior and pure spirits enjoy pleasant fragrances. Since the Prophet Muhammad (PBUH) regularly encountered angels and received revelations, he refrained from eating foods that had strong flavors that repel angels, such as onion and garlic.

Angels' worships are equivalent like fard (obligatory). Voluntary worships (supererogatory) are no question for them. Supererogatory worship is an award for humans. A Hadith al Qudsi says as follows; "My servants would gain my love by performing supererogatory worships".

Since they have no tendency to perform bad deeds, getting thawab (reward) is no question for angels by avoiding things forbidden by Allah.

They are classified into three types: those who worship, those associated with nature, and those associated with humans.

Worshiping angels are constantly repeating the names of God Almighty, glorifying Him, and blessing Him with all of His perfect features.

Nature-related angels are in charge of regulating the cosmos and implementing divine laws that keep nature in order. They supervise and watch the manifestations of Allah's will and might in nature.

Gabriel (PBUH) is the most significant in terms of Angels relating to humans. His role is to communicate divine revelation to prophets. As a result, he is also known as the angel of revelation. The closest angel to Allah is Gabriel (PBUH). Do not think of it as material distance. Allah is freed from space.

The Prophet (PBUH) said,

"If Allah loves a person, He calls Gabriel and says to him, 'Allah loves so and so, O Gabriel love him.' So, Gabriel loves him and then will make an announcement in the Heavens: 'Allah loves so and-so therefore you love him too.' So all the dwellers of the Heavens start to love him, and then he is granted the consent of the people on the earth."

Here I want to talk about the angels who participated in the wars:

The most famous battle in which the angels came to help the believers is undoubtedly the battle of Badr. Well, if the angels helped Muslims in the battle of Badr, why was the death toll so low in those battles?

If the descent of angels were only to kill the unbelievers, even one angel would be enough to destroy all the unbelievers. In the battle of Badr, the angels came as a miracle and to calm the hearts of the believers and raise their morale. Angels are beings belonging to the realm of the hereafter. It is a great miracle that they come and fight on the same side with the believers.

Undoubtedly, the battles of Badr and Uhud are a broad subject with many wisdoms. I will not go into these matters. I will suffice with only one reason for the loss of the Battle of Uhud.

*Why were the Muslims defeated in the Battle of Uhud?*

One of its many reasons and wisdom is this: There were many people among the polytheists at that time, such as Khalid bin Walid (R.A), Amr bin As (R.A). Divine wisdom has given this victory to these people, who will take their place in the ranks of the Companions and render great services in the future, as a reward for their good deeds in the future. In addition, divine wisdom did not completely break their dignity by taking into account their glorious and honorable future. The Companions of the past were defeated by the Companions of the future.

# Since God has Infinite Power, why did He Create Angels?

Why were angels created?

The word angel should not remind us of a specific species. When we say animals and plants, we do not think of a single species. Likewise, there are varieties of angels. Not even a drop of rain falls on its own. There is an angel assigned to every raindrop. And the type of that angel is not the same as the angel who is delegated to the sun, MilkyWay, and the throne of Allah.

Allah is not in need of anything He has created, nor is He in need of His angels. The works of angels are not helping Allah, but worshiping Him.

It is the people who apply the law in the social life order. Those who apply the laws of the universe are angels, who are the servants of Allah.

However, nothing in the Universe has any real influence except Allah. Therefore, angels have no creative work. They are at their place of duty to contemplate the magnificence of the works of Allah's power and to glorify Him consciously. It is the infinite divine power that holds the reins of these laws.

Most of the angels only glorify Allah. Angels, who are responsible for maintaining the order in the universe, both deal with the laws of nature and glorify Allah. These angels are called labor angels, and they are personally involved in the implementation of the laws governing every being, from particles to planets. However, everything is under Allah's control. Angels are only applauders and supervisors of divine action.

It is not possible for humans and jinn to see all the magnificent works in all parts of the universe. Angels can be found all over the universe and they can see and contemplate all the wonderful works.

Mountains, rivers, flowers, gardens. Magma, Planets, stars, galaxies, colorful nebulae. Pearls and corals at the bottom of the sea. The fish do not understand anything by watching them. A cow cannot appreciate the art in flowers by looking at them. These magnificent arts require conscious beings who will remember Allah, appreciate and express their admiration. These conscious beings are angels.

While the angels are operating the magnificent laws of Allah, they admire the names and attributes of Allah. Each artist wants to have audiences who will understand and appreciate the delicacy and beauty of his art.

Humans and jinn are insufficient to see many of the art that should be appreciated in this universe exhibition. For this reason, Allah has created angels, who can be found anywhere from the core of the earth to the seven heavens, so that they can watch and appreciate the arts in the universe exhibition. Angels, on the one hand, while doing their jobs, on the other hand, they watch the names and attributes of Allah with admiration.

Allah has created angels to see the perfect names and arts that belong to Him.

When an artist creates an art, he wants to see the beauty in it. Just like that, God watches His angels, who are His own art. The high talent, beauty and perfection in angels belong to Allah.

God watches His angels working, thus watches the activities of His names, the arts of His mercy, the magnificence of His dominance... There is a sacred pleasure in this that is worthy of His own exalted self. The pleasure and joy of God are not like ours. We are incapable of understanding.

God does everything himself. However, in order not to harm His dignity and greatness, He has made the reasons a veil. Angels and causes are veils. Since I have covered these issues in my previous books and not to distract the subject, I am ending it here.

# Conclusion

Allah wants man to strive. For a work to be successful, the necessary reasons must be fulfilled. It is only God who determines the outcome. When our mother Mary gave birth, Allah told her to shake the date branch towards herself so that ripe fresh dates would fall on her. This date tree was dry and had no fruit. The season was winter. Hazrat Meryem pulled the branch of the tree towards herself and shook it, and Allah gave that dry tree both branches and fresh dates. There are many wisdoms in this miracle. I just want to draw your attention to one. Allah has the power to give dates to the tree, even if Hazrat Maryam does not touch the tree. But He asks her to take an action. This is how man fulfills causes. Reasons cannot give a person anything. Allah gives. However, man must fulfill the causes and expect the result from Allah.

Knife doesn't cut. Fire does not burn. It is Allah who cuts and burns. The knife did not cut prophet Ismael(PBUH). The fire did not burn Abraham(PBUH). Jesus (PBUH) was born without a father.

Let's consider the issue of God's help in wars in this context.

If believers fulfill the reasons but the reasons are insufficient, Allah will help them. But God wants us to fulfill the reasons. If non-Muslims fulfill the reasons, they win. This is how God's law works. If non-Muslims who fulfill their reasons completely get spoiled and oppress Muslims by going beyond the limits, then Allah may/will help Muslims.

Also, the help of Allah comes because of the trouble taken in the way of Allah. It's like Yavuz Sultan Selim crossing the Sinai Desert.

Muslims must take up arms and always be ahead of the enemy in the arms race. There is no peace without war. War is bad. But what do you think would happen if the Muslims burned their swords and said there was no more war? The enemy would not stop. The enemy would attack more brutally. For this reason, the Islamic army must be strong and ensure world peace.

# Don't miss out!

Visit the website below and you can sign up to receive emails whenever ahmet yazici publishes a new book. There's no charge and no obligation.

https://books2read.com/r/B-A-XNWH-FTCBC

**BOOKS 2 READ**

Connecting independent readers to independent writers.

Did you love *Armies of the Heavens: Divine Help in Wars*? Then you should read *The Return of Jesus: Conquest of Rome*[1] by ahmet yazici!

Jesus Christ is going to be among us again, for sure. There are inevitably some signs of this blessed person's coming. So what are these signs? What causes Jesus Christ to be sent again on earth? How do we recognize him? What will change in the world after he arrives? While answering these questions, I have addressed some other individuals related to Jesus Christ, and some signs of doom.

---

1. https://books2read.com/u/bOykAK

2. https://books2read.com/u/bOykAK

When talking about Jesus Christ, the indispensable word is the great antichrist. I specifically discussed the great Antichrist.Who were the antichrists who came in the 20th century?Which states sided with the antichrist and which sided with Jesus Christ in the 20th century?How will the struggle between Prophet Jesus (PBUH) and the Antichrist be in this century?

There are various comings of Jesus Christ (PBUH) in the end times. The most important of these is that he comes down from the sky himself.When you read this work, you will understand the truth and secret of the coming of Jesus.

# About the Author

Ahmet Yazici lives in Turkey with his parents and brother. He likes to write non-fiction Islamic works that prove the truths of faith in a rational way and fiction works (primarily fantasy fiction).

www.ingramcontent.com/pod-product-compliance
Lightning Source LLC
Chambersburg PA
CBHW051300160726
47994CB00003B/1252